# Being a Server Today

*A resource for all who assist
at the liturgy*

Brendan Clover
and
Chris Verity

*Illustrated by Fabian Heller*

CANTERBURY
PRESS
Norwich

© Text: Brendan Clover and Chris Verity 2005
© Illustrations: Fabian Hellier 2005

First published in 2005 by the Canterbury Press Norwich
(a publishing imprint of Hymns Ancient & Modern Limited,
a registered charity)
St Mary's Works, St Mary's Plain,
Norwich, Norfolk NR3 3BH

www.scm-canterburypress.co.uk

British Library Cataloguing-in-Publication data

A catalogue record for this book is available
from the British Library

ISBN 1-85311-638-6

Typeset by Rowland Phototypesetting Ltd
Bury St Edmunds, Suffolk
Printed in the UK by CPI Bookmarque, Croydon, CR0 4TD

# Contents

We are the servants of the servants of God.

*St Gregory*

# Introduction

Why should you be thinking of offering yourself as a server in the Church, or why should you be continuing with it? For the sake of the one who came among us as 'one who serves' – for love of Jesus Christ himself. Jesus gave us an example of service as, at the Last Supper, he laid aside his garments, wrapped a towel around himself, and washed and dried his disciples' feet. He taught the disciples that mutual service is the hallmark of authentic Christian life. In the Gospels, time after time he hammers home the point – don't be as people in the world are; to follow me is to lay down your life, to die in order to be born again. The server has the same vocation as any other Christian – to seek to become one whose discipleship is costly and self-giving.

To love and to be valued are the two most important things in life. In the Christian community we should know this instinctively. Every ministry in the Church must be valued, for all of us have a part to play in the building up of the body of Christ.

Often those who work behind the scenes can feel undervalued. Saint Paul says that 'we reap what we sow' (Galatians 6.7) and what he means is that the quality of the end result is dependent on the quality and thoroughness of the preparation for it. This is true of everything, and it is true of the liturgy, because the word 'liturgy' means the 'work of the people'. The liturgy is the public expression of the Church and the most immediate contact many will have with the local Christian community, and so those who have a function in that work need to be valued in a special way.

The server represents the Christian community. In my teenage years I would often serve at the early Saturday Mass and many a time there would be just the priest, the angels, and me! What a privilege to represent the people of God as I offered the priest the bread and the wine, the gifts of the people of God, for the Eucharist. Because the server stands in the Holy of Holies with the priest representing the people of God, he or she must be a person of prayer and devotion.

On ceremonial occasions the server has a high profile in the liturgy and the highest standards of dress and decorum should rightly be expected of him or her. Our attitude to what we are doing is communicated by attention to detail, by the standards of our dress and appearance, by inward disposition. What does Saint Paul say? That God accepts our weaknesses and failings, but that is no excuse not to offer the best we have.

In this book we shall look at the following aspects of being a server: preparing for the service; the life of prayer; and ceremonial occasions. We are going to be 'gender-inclusive', so where we write 'he' and 'him' it includes 'she' and 'her'! We hope we will have something to offer you, in whatever situation you may encounter in the Church of God.

# 2

# People

There is much talk these days in the Church about 'collaborative ministry'. Underpinning this idea is the image in St Paul of the Church as Christ's body. In the letter to the Romans he writes:

> For as in one body we have many members, and all the members do not have the same function, so we, though many, are one body in Christ, and individually members one of another. Having gifts that differ according to the grace given to us, let us use them . . . (Romans 12.4–6a)

The server is part of the team that enables the worship to take place. The function of the priest, the president of the Eucharist, is to make sure that the various parts of the liturgy come together to make a whole that is satisfying and worthy as the worship of Almighty God. So the server will look to the priest for guidance and leadership, and will seek to cultivate a kind of intuitive rapport with the priest as he or she gets to understand more deeply the liturgy, and the movement of the liturgy, and the variety of the Christian year. But as the representative of the congregation the server has a duty to relate to the people of God in the congregation and at the Eucharist. It is a relationship cultivated in respect and kindness, and in a proper degree of humility. Keep before you the image of Jesus washing his disciples' feet and you can't go far wrong. It used to be said of children that they 'should be seen but not heard' and there is a sense in which the server has done his or her job well if it can be said of them that 'they were not noticed'. This will mean that the server has become part of the work of the liturgy in such a way as to be totally submersed in it, living the ritual from the inside out.

Being part of a team brings with it a series of responsibilities and this sense of teamwork is fundamental to the ministry of a server. To be part of a team implies valuing one another, accepting the gifts other people bring, seeing them as complementary to one's own gifts and strengths. In this way we become 'members one of another'.

# 3

# Vocation

Now to do this, to learn how to accept and value one another, we need to cultivate a kind of inner stillness. We need to be Mary and Martha in the Gospel story (Luke 10.38–42). Like the priest, you are likely to be busy before the Eucharist making sure that everything is ready for the celebration, and during the Eucharist, because there are many practical things that need to be done and ceremonial details that you need to remember, you are not going to be free to participate in the same way as an ordinary member of the congregation. You may find that going to church to serve brings with it a sense of being under pressure to deliver of your best so as not to 'let the side down'. Because of this you need to cultivate a kind of inner stillness. You need time to be Mary as well as time to be Martha, time to sit at the Lord's feet. Paying attention to your own personal spiritual life is fundamental. Perhaps you could attend a weekday service as well as one on Sunday and not be pushed into serving at it! Could you find ten minutes each day or each week to 'be still and know that I am God' (Psalm 46.10)? How about saying the Office of Compline quietly on a Saturday night when you go to bed as a form of preparation for Holy Communion, or join others to do so? It would repay you many times to do so. After all, given that the server stands so close to the holy things of God in the sanctuary, we do well to cultivate a sense of the Holy in our lives.

# 4

# The Church Building

Many church buildings, especially if they are medieval, are cruciform, built in the shape of the cross. These buildings have a nave; transepts; a quire, chancel; and there may be aisles either side of the nave. There may also be a small chapel, or chapels, where weekday services take place. Often when you stand at the back of such a church and look down the length of it to the high altar you will notice that the quire or chancel is at a slight angle to the nave. This is meant to represent the head of Christ on the cross, leaning to one side. All of these spaces inside the church may be used liturgically, as may areas outside the church, such as the churchyard or garden where the New Fire may be lit on Easter Day, or a church hall where the people may assemble for the Palm Sunday procession. Some cultures use outdoor spaces for worship considerably more than we do. In Mexico, for instance, there is the custom of gathering in the graveyard on All Souls' Day for a party that consists of eating *pan de muerto*, the bread of the dead!

The fundamental principle behind the liturgical renewal that has come to fruition in *Common Worship* in the Church of England is that the Eucharist is the action of the people of God within which the priest and everyone present have a part to play. This new emphasis on the Eucharist as the joint activity of the people of God has come to be expressed in many places by liturgical reordering. In the old days the priest stood at the high altar with his back to the people, standing as it were as an intermediary between the congregation and God, offering the sacrifice of the Eucharist. This image spoke of a God who is 'other', 'transcendent'. The new emphasis is on a God who is among us, 'immanent', 'tangible', and to express this a new altar has been brought closer to the people, perhaps at the head of the nave or in a quire where choir stalls have been removed.

This 'nave' altar is going to be the focus of your duties as a server. In fact these 'new' ideas are not new at all – the oldest churches were like Roman law courts or basilicas, where the judges sat behind the table, with two desks or ambos for the defence and opposition lawyers. When the Church took over this form of building the bishops and clergy took the seats of the judges behind the altar table, and the ambos became the places for reading the lessons and proclaiming the gospel. The writer of Ecclesiastes was right: 'there is nothing new under the sun'!

The altar, whether old or new, is likely to be marked with five crosses cut into its surface. These five crosses remind us of the five wounds of Christ on the cross, the

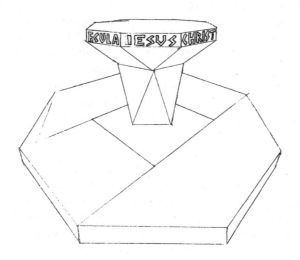

holes made by the nails and the wound made by the spear that pierced his side. In medieval times the ceremony for consecrating an altar was long and elaborate, involving washing the altar, as in Baptism, anointing the altar with Holy Chrism, as in Confirmation, and burning incense on the altar, before covering it with cloths and offering the sacrifice of the Eucharist. Likewise until recently everything that was to be placed on the altar was set aside for its purpose by prayers of blessing, especially the chalice and paten, which were dedicated by the bishop, and all altars contained fragments of bones of the saints (relics) which were sealed into it. The altar is a principal symbol of the presence of Christ in the Church, and is to be treated always with the utmost respect. It is not a sideboard or a shelf to leave books or anything else on, and when approaching it, it is customary to bow profoundly. When we bow in the sanctuary it is not to the cross, but to the altar.

Because Jesus Christ is the Light of the World, candles are placed on or near the altar for the Eucharist and for Evening Prayer. There may be as many as six candles on the altar, with two standard or floor candles. Designs for these have changed significantly over the past few years because now the celebrant stands behind the altar facing the people and it is important for him to be visible. Some churches produce a seventh candle when the bishop comes on his visits, but this practice appears to be dying out. The important thing is that the altar should not look cluttered, that it is covered with a decent white cloth, and that it is treated with dignity and respect.

A cross may stand near the altar. When the Eucharist takes place with the celebrant facing west, toward the people, it cannot stand on the altar as it would obscure the celebrant. Many churches use the processional cross as the altar cross, carrying it in at the beginning of the service in the entrance procession, and taking it away again in

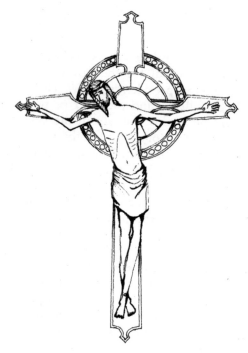

procession at the end of the service. This cross does not need to be placed centrally, but it does need a stand or hole in the ground so it remains safely upright, and it must be clearly seen. The cross may or may not hold a figure of the crucified Christ, or of Christ the High Priest clothed in Eucharistic vestments, and if your church has more than one, they may be suitable for different seasons of the year. A small cross or crucifix may be placed on the altar to aid the devotion of the priest.

Your priest will have given thought to where the readings are to be read. This may be a fixed lectern or movable *legilium* (reading desk). The Gospel reading may be read either from this place or in the midst of the congregation after a Gospel procession. The Book of the Gospels may be carried in the entrance procession by the priest or a deacon and placed on the altar until the Gospel is read, then placed back on the altar to remind us that we feed at the table of God's Word as well as his Sacrament.

Nowadays it is usual for the priest to preside at the Eucharist from the president's chair. This is sometimes positioned centrally behind the altar or to one side, and the priest will be at this chair from the beginning of the service until the Offertory, and for the prayers and blessing after Holy Communion. The seating for the servers will relate to the altar, the president's chair, the lectern and the pulpit.

Near the altar is the credence table, on which are placed the chalice and paten, the breadbox, the cruets, and the lavabo jug and basin.

On the high altar, or in a side chapel, is a receptacle in which is reserved the consecrated bread (and sometimes wine) for the communion of the sick and housebound. This may be called a tabernacle – reminding us of the Old Testament teaching that God has 'tabernacled' among his people, made his home with them – or an aumbry (another word for safe or cupboard) often set in the wall, or even a free-standing sacrament house. This is also a place generally set aside for private prayer, and a place where silence is encouraged. After the Sunday Eucharist, the priest may replenish the wafers of bread in the receptacle of the reserved sacrament, so that the connection is made between the Sunday congregation and the individuals who receive Communion at home. In some churches, when the door of the aumbry is opened, a server rings a bell to let people know that they should be quiet and prayerful. Some churches have a service called Benediction or Devotions which involves the placing of the ciborium or monstrance containing the Blessed Sacrament on the altar as a focus for prayer and adoration. We'll say more about that later in Chapter 9.

Finally, the font in medieval churches is usually near the door. This reminds us that Baptism marks the entrance of an individual into the sacramental life of the Church and the mystical body of Christ. As it is much more usual now for Baptism to be administered in the course of the Sunday Eucharist the font may have been moved to a place closer to the altar so that the congregation can see what is going on more easily. If it is by the entrance to the church you may well be part of a procession to the font for the sacrament of Baptism. This may also take place in the course of the Easter Day services, which in ancient times was the day for Baptism. Nowadays we also renew our Baptismal vows and are sprinkled with the water of Baptism.

# 5

# The Sacristy

The sacristy is the 'behind the scenes' room where much preparation for the service takes place. It is also the place where you and the clergy robe for services, and where various items are stored and kept safe. It may contain a vestment press, a cupboard with several drawers for vestments of different colours, a safe and a sink that drains to earth. The sacristy needs to be well ordered and kept tidy and not a dumping ground!

---

**Liturgical Colours**

In the medieval Church there were various local uses which determined liturgical colour. In England the foremost of these was the Use of Sarum, which used blue for Advent and red for Ordinary Time.
 These are the current colours and their symbolism.

**Gold –**   festivals, especially Christmas, Easter, Christ the King.
*Gold is symbolic of glory, exuberance, celebration, and resurrection.*

**White –**   The Sundays of the Christmas and Easter seasons; Trinity Sunday; Corpus Christi; All Saints' Day; feasts of Our Lady[1] and the saints.

*White is symbolic of joy, exuberance, celebration, resurrection, victory, purity, innocence.*

**Red** – Palm Sunday and Good Friday; Pentecost; feasts of martyr saints; Holy Cross Day; the Kingdom season.
*Red is symbolic of the Holy Spirit, the suffering of Christ, of the Apostles, the blood of martyrdom; also the royal colour given as a sign of victory.*

**Purple** – Advent and Lent[2]; All Souls' Day; requiem Eucharists.
*Purple is symbolic of sorrow, mourning, repentance, penance.*

**Rose pink** – the Third Sunday of Advent and Fourth Sunday of Lent as an alternative to purple.
*Rose is symbolic of subdued joy and it is used on the Sundays which occur as midpoints in the penitential seasons. The Fourth Sunday of Lent is also known as Mothering Sunday.*

**Black/Grey** – sometimes used for requiems.
*Black is symbolic of mourning and death.*

**Green** – Ordinary Time: Sundays and all weekdays not saints' days.
*Green is symbolic of hope, everlasting life, and fidelity.*

1 Occasionally blue vestments are worn for Feasts of Our Lady.
2 Some churches have Lenten array, a kind of unbleached linen.

## Vestments

- **Chasuble** – the outer garment of the priest at the Eucharist. It began life as a simple cloak, but has been restricted to bishops and priests for the celebration of the Eucharist since the eighth century. It has evolved across the centuries into different shapes, but nowadays has reverted to a more original cloak-like shape and the full-cut Gothic style is often preferred. Other shapes you may come across are 'fiddle back', where the front of the vestment is the shape of a violin, or conical.
- **Dalmatic** – the outer garment of the deacon at the Eucharist. In AD 322 Pope Sylvester granted the dalmatic to the order of deacons. Before that it had been the garment of people of rank and privilege in civil society. The dalmatic is a vestment open on each side with wide sleeves and marked with two vertical stripes.

It is always the colour of the celebrant's chasuble and made of the same material.

- **Tunicle** – a variant of the dalmatic, worn by those who were sub-deacons, or those who performed the function of sub-deacon at a Eucharist celebrated with priest and deacon. It is generally less ornamented than the dalmatic, but may be identical. The crucifer may wear the tunicle.

- **Stole** – a long strip of fabric worn by the priest and the deacon. They receive the stole at ordination and always wear it for the Eucharist and for other sacramental services. Some clergy wear them for funerals and even as 'choir dress'. The priest wears the stole round the back of the neck with each of the two ends falling the same length in front. The deacon wears the stole from the left shoulder, across the breast to the right hip, where it is tied or fastened. The stoles that are worn

with the Eucharistic vestments are of the same fabric and the same colour. The early writers of the Church attach to the stole the symbolism of service, of Christ washing the disciples' feet, and the deacon wearing the stole over the left shoulder is a reminder of the Roman custom of the slave wearing a cloth for his master over his left arm.

- **Alb** – worn over cassocks, these long white garments are reminiscent of the white baptismal garments worn by the elect in the Revelation of St John the Divine:

> After this I looked, and there was a great multitude that no one could count, from every nation, from all tribes and peoples and languages, standing before the throne and before the Lamb, robed in white, with palm branches in their hands. They cried out in a

loud voice, saying, 'Salvation belongs to our God who is seated on the throne, and to the Lamb!' (Revelation 7.9–10)

In fact the alb was the ordinary dress of a Roman citizen. It was worn with a tunic or cloak on top. Pope Sylvester introduced the long-sleeved alb that has remained in use until the present day. The alb is usually white or cream, and it should be full length.

- The alb may have a square or round neck, under which may be worn the **amice**, a rectangular piece of cloth with two linen or cotton strings at the upper corners by which it is fastened in place; and around the waist the alb is secured by the **girdle** or **cincture**.
- Other 'cassock albs' tend to be of heavier material than the alb with an integral hood or capuche. Some servers wear albs rather than cassock and surplice or cotta.

The Eucharistic vestments are laid out ready for the service like this:

- The chasuble or dalmatic is laid out first on the vestment press or a table.
- The stole is laid out next in the shape of an alpha, the first letter in the Greek alphabet, because Christ is the beginning.
- The girdle or cincture is laid out next in the shape of an omega, the last letter in the Greek alphabet, because Christ will be the end of all things.
- The alb is laid out next so that it can be put on easily.
- The amice, if worn, is laid as a cover over everything else with the tabs folded inwards in an X, the shape of a St Andrew's cross.

As the vestments are put on the priest may say prayers which describe the symbolism of each garment. You can find a version of these prayers in Chapter 13.

- **Cope** – a richly ornamented cloak with a hood on the back. It is worn over the alb or cassock and surplice, and it is not reserved to the clergy though it is rarely worn by laypeople. The cope is worn for processions, for Solemn Evensong, for Benediction, and by the bishop for Confirmation when there is no Eucharist. A purple cope may be worn by the priest for the Commendation of the departed at a funeral.

- **Mitre** – worn by the bishop with his cope or chasuble. Abbots and abbesses may also wear the mitre in their monasteries. Bishops have been wearing mitres since the twelfth century. The mitre symbolizes the flames of Pentecost announcing the outpouring of the Holy Spirit and therefore of the apostolic ministry. Often the mitre is elaborately decorated, but the bishop will also have a simple mitre that is worn at funerals and on Good Friday.

- **Cassock** – the usual uniform for servers and clergy. It is worn to ankle length. The cassock is usually black, but

other colours are also found according to custom. You should look after your cassock. Wax is easily removed with some kitchen roll and a hot iron, and cassocks should be cleaned on a regular basis.

• The **surplice** or **cotta** is worn over the cassock. Both derive from the alb. By the eleventh century the surplice was required for all liturgical functions if one was not vested in the alb as the celebrant. Thus the surplice is one of the Church's oldest items of vesture, having been in use without a break for more than a thousand years. The surplice may have either a square-cut neck or a rounded neck. It may have bell-shaped sleeves or long full sleeves. The cotta (named from the Italian verb for 'cut' or 'shorten') is generally shorter with square-cut sleeves. It may have box pleats, lace embroidery, or designs worked into the fabric at the bottom of the garment and the sleeves. Whatever is worn in your church, dignity and uniformity are imperative. You can't behave as a team if you don't look like one!

## Vessels

• The **paten** and **chalice** are the principal vessels at Holy Communion. They will invariably be made of silver or gold, or silver or gold plate. When wine is poured into a silver or gold chalice, the antiseptic action of the alcohol is enhanced. Since many people will drink from the one cup this is important! This is also the reason why a recent trend of producing chalice and paten from pottery or glass has come in for some heavy criticism. Your church will probably possess several chalices and patens, the gifts of forebears.

Usually a verger, the sacristan or the priest will prepare the chalice and paten, but if you are asked to do so, first of all place over the chalice the purificator – the

folded rectangle of cloth used to cleanse it after Communion – then place the paten holding the priest's wafer over the purificator, then the pall (a cloth-covered cardboard square which is used to keep dust off the paten and is symbolic of the stone that was rolled away from the tomb of Jesus), then the corporal (from the Latin *corpus* or body – the cloth on which will be placed the sacred body and blood of Jesus). Some churches still use the chalice veil, which goes over the pall, and the burse, which contains the corporal. These are made of fabric and match the vestments.

- The **ciborium** is of a similar shape to the chalice, but it has a covering or lid. This is the vessel that holds large

numbers of hosts or breads, and therefore will be used at the principal services. The reserved hosts in the tabernacle or aumbry will be kept in a ciborium.

- The **thurible** or **censer** is used in churches that use incense as part of their worship. A thurible is a metal bowl on chains with a cover that can be lifted up for the priest to put incense on hot charcoal tablets in the bowl. The hot charcoal makes the incense melt, and in melting it produces smoke and perfume as the resins dissolve in the heat. The rising of smoke is a sign of the prayers of the people of God rising to the throne of God, and of the importance we attach to the holy things of God, the altar, the cross, and the Sacrament itself. The bearer of the thurible, the thurifer, has the most difficult job on the serving team, and it has to be learnt, so don't be surprised if it takes you a while to get there!
- **Bells** are often used in the service. They are rung from the church tower to announce that an act of worship is about to take place, and at various points in the service: at the beginning as a signal for the people to stand and

when the priest lifts up the bread and the cup after the words of Jesus in the Eucharistic prayer. Some churches have gongs instead of bells for these moments, except at the beginning of the service when the sacring bell, a small bell near the sacristy door, is used.

- In churches that have Benediction or Devotions a **monstrance** may be used. Its name comes from the Latin verb *monstrare* which means to show. These may be simple or very ornate, but each will contain a glass capsule, called a lunette, within which the Sacrament is fixed so that it can be seen by the priest and people and focused upon for prayer and adoration.

- Some churches will also possess a **bucket** used for **holy water**, and a **sprinkler** (*aspergillum*). Such blessed water may be used at funerals, when the coffin is sprinkled as a reminder of Baptism, at weddings when the rings are being blessed, to bless crosses and other objects of devotion, and at the renewal of Baptismal vows at Easter. The priest may ask you to say the prayers for the blessing of holy water with him, and if he does, it is customary to make the sign of the cross on your forehead with the water at the end of the prayers. Your church may also have a holy water stoop near the main door where you can do the same thing when entering and leaving. Remember that 'in this sign we conquer'.

All these vestments and vessels may be kept in the sacristy along with the liturgical books, the altar books, and other resources. The sacristy may have a crucifix over the place where the priest vests for the Eucharist and even a small safe in which are kept the holy oils: the oil of Baptism; the oil of the sick; and the oil of chrism. Sometimes this safe has a purple fabric covering.

It is good to cultivate the habit of being silent in the sacristy before services begin. Remember the maxim: 'Before the service talk to God; during the service let God talk to you; after the service talk to one another.'

# 6

# The Liturgical Year

## Advent and Christmas

**Advent Sunday** is the first day of the new Christian year. The mood of the season is restrained, penitential, so purple is the liturgical colour. Advent comes from the Latin noun *adventus*, which means 'coming', so it is a time of preparation for the coming of the Christ child at Christmas (not the ecclesiastical equivalent to 'X shopping days before Christmas'). Some churches have an Advent wreath, which has five candles, four of them representing the four Sundays of Advent and their themes, and the fifth representing the birth of the Light of the World. Sometimes these candles are purple (one of them may be pink for the Third Sunday of Advent, when rose pink may be worn) but white will do. The candles are often lit at the main Sunday Eucharist, so you may need to be on hand to help with that. The season of Advent may also be marked by special services of carols and readings or penitential celebrations.

**Midnight Mass** is one of the most special services of the year, marking the birth of Christ and the angels' announcement to the shepherds. At this service the crib may be blessed and the Christ child placed in it by the priest. This may happen at the beginning or the end of the service. It may happen after an elaborate procession with carols and incense or more quietly to mark the awesome mystery we celebrate.

God made man in Palestine
lives today in bread and wine.

The **Christmas season** lasts from Christmas Day to the feast of the Presentation of Christ in the Temple (Candlemas) on 2 February or the Sunday nearest. The season has two stages, the time up until Epiphany (6 January) and the time after Epiphany. It is very sad that in many churches the season of Christmas after Boxing Day is virtually ignored: the January sales begin in the shops and everyone starts to think about New Year's resolutions and getting some weight off! But the days between Christmas and Epiphany are full of wonder as the Church celebrates Stephen, the first martyr, the Holy Innocents, St John the Evangelist, St Thomas Becket, the Holy Family, and the Circumcision of Christ. How grateful your parish priest would be if you showed some interest as a server in helping observe these days, and what a huge amount there is to be gained from it!

Often at the Epiphany Eucharist the gifts of gold, frankincense and myrrh are presented in the course of the service. (For further details of the services mentioned in this chapter, see Chapter 9.) The gift of gold reminds us that Christ is King, the gift of frankincense that he is God and the gift of myrrh (the oil used to embalm the dead) that he is to suffer and die for us. Again these gifts may be presented in a simple or a solemn manner according to local custom, but you will need to be on hand to help. In some churches the gift of gold is represented by a gold chalice; the gift of frankincense by incense burnt and offered; the gift of myrrh by the oil of the sick, which is also used to give the faithful the last rites.

With this feast the twelve days of Christmas come to a close and the theme changes to our contemplation of the childhood of Christ culminating in the **Presentation of Christ in the Temple**. Long before the Western Church had

Christmas Day, which began life as a secular festival of 'the birth day of the Sun', it had Epiphany or the 'manifestation of Christ to the Gentiles', which brought together the themes of the Visit of the Wise Men, the Baptism of Christ, and the first miracle at Cana in Galilee, all of these showing how Christ reveals something of God to the world, to you and to me.

On the Presentation of Christ in the Temple a Procession of Light is part of the service with the entire congregation carrying lighted candles. This can be at the beginning of the service, reminding us of the journey of the Holy Family to Jerusalem for that poignant meeting between Mary, Jesus, Simeon and Anna (Luke 2.22–39), or at the end of the service as a kind of bridge between the Christmas season and the forthcoming season of Lent (see Chapter 9). In fact in ancient times the procession was penitential in feel: the Emperor Maurice took part in it barefoot and until the reforms of the Roman Rite in 1968 the celebrant wore purple for the procession and white for the Mass. So the Procession on Candlemas day has always had a bittersweet feel to it. Think of it – we dare to carry the light of Christ but we all know how far we are from reflecting that light in the world, so we carry it unworthily.

## Lent

Lent begins on **Ash Wednesday.** Baptism and Confirmation were administered only at the Easter celebration in the early centuries of the Church, so Lent was the time for new Christians to be taught and examined in the faith. In the course of time it came to be seen that everyone could benefit from an extended preparation for Holy Week and Easter.

At the Eucharist on Ash Wednesday ashes made from burnt palms of the year before are placed on each person's forehead by the priest, who recites the words, 'Remember you are dust and to dust you will return', reminding us that our life is not ours but God's and that one day we shall lay it down. What we do with our lives on Earth then assumes so much more importance!

The season of Lent is one of penitence and challenge, time for taking stock of one's life, a chance to ask ourselves what is really important to us. We seek to grow closer to God and to our truest and deepest selves. This is no easy journey for it is the Way of the Cross. Some churches have Lenten array, which is colourless linen often embroidered with symbols of the Passion of Christ, and on **Passion Sunday**, the Fifth Sunday of Lent, the images and crosses in the church are covered with purple cloth as the season gathers intensity and the focus shifts towards Jerusalem and the final days of Our Lord's earthly life.

**Mothering Sunday**, however, is a bit of a let-up, a mid-point in the penitential season. It is so called because of an antiphon used in the propers of the day which refers to Jerusalem as 'mother of us all', but in Victorian times those whose work was in domestic service had a day off and went 'a-mothering', returning home to give flowers to their mothers and spend the day at home. As this is a day for some refreshment (Mothering Sunday's other name is Refreshment Sunday), pink is the colour for the vestments again. So rose pink is worn twice a year, the Third Sunday in Advent and Fourth Sunday in Lent, and it is not surprising many churches feel able to do without it. Perhaps people in your parish might give some pink vestments in thanksgiving for their mothers!

## Holy Week and Easter

Holy Week is the most important week in the Christian year. The liturgies of Holy Week are very ancient. They can be traced back at least to the pilgrimage a Spanish or Gallic nun, Egeria, made to the Holy Land in the fourth century. As the liturgies were devised at the sites of the events of the week, largely by St Cyril of Jerusalem, and as those sites were spread all over and outside the city of Jerusalem, it is no surprise that the services all contain significant processions (see Chapter 9), reminders of the journeys of Jesus during the last days of his earthly life.

Your church may have a series of 14 images or carvings of the **Stations of the Cross,** and in Lent a service of devotion may take place that is a journey around the church contemplating the journey of Our Lord to Calvary. That service is a good way of entering into the mystery of the passion and death of Jesus and of meditating on it. As a server you may even be called upon to help with it, by carrying the processional cross or a candle, but generally these days the service takes a less elaborate form with the priest in a cassock, cotta and purple stole leading the assembled throng.

**Palm Sunday** begins with a triumphant procession reminding us of the entrance of Jesus into the city of Jerusalem and the crowds greeting him by shouting 'Hosanna to the Son of David'. Wherever possible, palms are blessed at a place outside the church where the Gospel account of these happenings is read, and the servers, with incense (if it is used), cross and lights lead the people into the church singing 'All glory, laud and honour' or some other suitable hymn. The clergy may wear copes for this procession. Then the service changes in atmosphere and the readings and the Passion of Jesus take us to Good Friday and the cross. The Passion according to one of the Gospels is solemnly declaimed (without a Gospel procession on this occasion) and those who have shouted 'Hosanna!' find the words 'Crucify him!' on their lips.

On the morning of **Maundy Thursday** (or at some other

time in the first days of Holy Week) the bishop gathers with his priests and deacons, and others involved in the ministry of the Church, for a Eucharist (sometimes called the Chrism Mass) at which vows are renewed and the holy oils are blessed for use in the forthcoming year. This service has recently found its way back into the general practice of the Church of England along with the use of holy oil and you might think about attending it!

In the evening the Church celebrates the Liturgy of the Last Supper (see Chapter 9). This service often ends with a Procession of the Sacrament, reminding us of the journey of Jesus from the Upper Room at the end of the Last Supper to the Garden of Gethsemane. But the Eucharist on this night may also contain a re-enactment of the washing of the disciples' feet, when the celebrant takes off the chasuble, wraps a towel around himself, and washes the feet of twelve members of the congregation. You may be one such representative and you will certainly feel those words of Jesus, 'I came not to be served, but to serve, and to give up my life for many' (Matthew 20.28). In some churches, once the Procession of the Sacrament has taken place, servers and the clergy return to strip the altars of their vesture and to wash them with water and wine. This has a practical as well as a spiritual significance, for Good Friday and Holy Saturday are the only days on which the Eucharist may not be celebrated and therefore the only days the altars can be washed and left to dry, but it reminds us too of the words in Psalm 22 prefiguring the Passion of Christ:

But as for me, I am a worm and no man,
scorned by all and despised by the people.
All who see me laugh me to scorn;
they curl their lips and wag their heads, saying,
'He trusted in the Lord; let him deliver him;
let him deliver him, if he delights in him.'

But it is you that took me out of the womb
and laid me safe upon my mother's breast.
On you was I cast ever since I was born;
you are my God even from my mother's womb.
Be not far from me, for trouble is near at hand
and there is none to help.
Mighty oxen come around me;
fat bulls of Bashan close me in on every side.
They gape upon me with their mouths,
as it were a ramping and a roaring lion.
I am poured out like water;
all my bones are out of joint;
my heart has become like wax
melting in the depths of my body.
My mouth is dried up like a potsherd;
my tongue cleaves to my gums;
you have laid me in the dust of death.
For the hounds are all about me,
the pack of evildoers close in on me;
they pierce my hands and my feet.
I can count all my bones;
they stand staring and looking upon me.
They divide my garments among them;
they cast lots for my clothing.
Be not far from me, O Lord;
you are my strength; hasten to help me.
Deliver my soul from the sword,
my poor life from the power of the dog.
Save me from the lion's mouth,
from the horns of wild oxen.
You have answered me! (Psalm 22.6–21)

The Liturgy of the Lord's Death on **Good Friday** is one of
the most powerful of all the services in the Church's year.
It begins with the entrance of the servers and sacred min-
isters in silence. The celebrant wears a red chasuble; the

servers do not carry candles or the cross. When the sanctuary or the head of the nave is reached all kneel and the clergy may prostrate themselves on the floor as a sign of the devastation and desolation of the day. What else can we do before the mystery of the love of God? 'O happy fault, O necessary sin of Adam that brought for us so great a redeemer' (from the Exultet).

The service continues with the prophet Isaiah's suffering servant, and the Passion of St John, solemnly proclaimed. No candles are used for the Passion, and there are no Gospel responses. After the Passion come the Solemn Prayers, formal intercessions for the Church and for the world God loved so much he gave his only Son. Next come two processional movements. After the prayers a cross is brought into the church. It may be accompanied by two acolytes with candles and be placed before the people so that they may come and venerate the cross (see Chapter 9). Various traditions exist for this – some kneel before it for a moment, some kiss the foot of the cross, others may place a votive candle there. At this point we seek to take the cross into ourselves.

> Were the whole realm of nature mine,
> that were an offering far too small.
> Love so amazing, so divine,
> demands my soul, my life, my all.
>
> (Isaac Watts)

Then the celebrant and servers collect the Sacrament for communion (see Chapter 9). For centuries the Eucharist has not been celebrated on Good Friday, and though it is not prohibited in the Church of England, it seems more appropriate to receive the bread and wine consecrated on Maundy Thursday, for in a sense these two services are in fact one. The Sacrament is brought to the altar accompanied by two acolytes with their candles, the Lord's Prayer is said, communion is distributed, and the service ends dramatically. All depart in silence.

**Holy Saturday** is the day the Church prays especially for the departed as Jesus rests in the tomb. It is likely to be a busy day in the church, particularly if the Easter Vigil takes places after sundown on Holy Saturday. There is so much to get ready for Easter: the altars to dress, flowers to arrange, preparations for the liturgy. It is a day of waiting, of expectancy and some hard work!

The **Easter Vigil** is the most important service of the entire year, and Easter is the Queen of Feasts. All is sumptuous, extravagant, for this is the day of resurrection. Wherever possible, a fire is kindled and blessed outside the church. This is the New Fire of Easter and is said to have come into the rite via St Patrick. From this fire the Paschal candle is lit. It bears the cross, the letters alpha and omega, the year, and the five wounds of Christ at the points and middle of the cross. This is one occasion when incense should be *de rigueur*!

The Paschal candle is carried into church and the procession of the Light of Christ (*Lumen Christi*) halts three times. At each halt the deacon intones, 'The Light of Christ', and the rest respond, 'Thanks be to God.' The congregation light their candles. The Paschal candle may be honoured with incense. In ancient times one of the duties of the deacon was to write a text for the Exultet. The form we have now may date from the time of St Ambrose, who died in AD 397. It is a profoundly beautiful poetic description of the work of redemption and a song in praise of the light of Christ. We then listen to the story of our redemption from the Jewish scriptures, and then rise to sing the Easter Gloria. The Gloria has not been heard in the church since before Lent, so it may be accompanied by fanfares, bells, football rattles, dustbin lids, whatever you can get your hands on! This is a time for some exuberance!

During or before the Gloria, the altar candles may be lit,

lights turned on, veils removed, sanctuary lamps lit, etc. All should be done to heighten the drama that lets us know 'The Lord is risen' – 'He is risen indeed!'

Since Baptism has been administered at this service since ancient times it is appropriate that it should be now. At the very least the people go to the font where water is blessed and all renew the vows they made at their baptism. The hand candles, which have been extinguished after the Exultet, are lit again for the renewal of baptismal vows as a sign of our Christian calling: 'Shine as lights in the world to the glory of God the Father!'[1] Then the people go to the altar to celebrate the Paschal Feast. Nothing can convey the excitement of this service other than your attending one which is done well. You won't need anything else to convince you that the liturgy can change our lives!

Eastertide continues until the feast of **Pentecost**. Like the season of Christmas it is in two parts, the time up to **Ascension Day**, and the time after, when the theme is oriented towards the coming of the Holy Spirit, the Advocate. Ascension Day may be celebrated with special solemnity in your parish and it is a holy day of obligation. You will want to make your communion.

## Ordinary Time

The time from the Feast of Candlemas until Ash Wednesday, and from Pentecost to Advent, is known variously as Ordinary Time, the Sundays after Trinity, the Sundays after Pentecost, even the Sundays *per annum* (Latin for 'through the year'). One of the three synoptic Gospels is read Sunday by Sunday and we learn of the deeds and teaching of Jesus. The feasts of the Holy

1 Words from 'Sending Out' in *Common Worship: Initiation Services*.

Trinity, Corpus Christi, the Blessed Virgin Mary, All Saints, and All Souls or the Commemoration of the Faithful Departed all occur during Ordinary Time and you will observe them in your church in your own way. The last Sunday of the liturgical year is the feast of Christ the King and we pray that his kingdom may come 'on earth as it is in heaven'.

The liturgical year has so much to teach us, and we don't need to invent or reinvent it! The server's task is to create the space where the mysteries we celebrate can draw the people of God into a deep relationship with him, so that we all learn how to be better disciples, how to live as followers of Christ, as the baptized people of God. That is quite a challenge and a responsibility, and an enormous opportunity.

# 7

# The Serving Team

## Master of Ceremonies

The master of ceremonies (MC) is in charge of the serving team. He should always be an experienced server, able to think on his feet in emergencies. He should know exactly what every other server should be doing at any particular time, and be able to put mistakes right without making it obvious. He should also be completely familiar with the duties of the celebrant, concelebrants and deacon. Some knowledge of the music at any particular service is an advantage.

It is preferable if the MC does not have any duties that anchor him in a specific place – such as holding the book – but this is frequently not possible. Above all, the MC must avoid being officious or flamboyant. He must be able to 'run' the service without appearing to do so.

## Acolytes

The acolytes and crucifer normally follow the thurifer in procession if there is one – otherwise they lead it. If following they should maintain a sensible gap from the thurifer (about five or six feet), if only to avoid the possibility of physical damage!

Apart from carrying candles in processions and at the Gospel, acolytes serve at the altar, normally being responsible for bringing the elements, the corporal and the vessels to the altar. In many churches they receive the gifts of bread, wine and water from the people, at the end of the Offertory procession. Ciboria and chalices should be placed on the altar alongside the corporal (unless directed otherwise); extra care must be taken if the chalice already has wine in it. If a chalice has a pall on it, it is best to carry the chalice by its stem in the right hand, with the left hand placed on top of the pall. Always find out beforehand whether the pall is to be left on the altar or returned to the credence table – celebrants often have strong views on this question. When presenting cruets, it is best to hand the wine to the priest first, then transfer the water from the left to the right hand, and then receive the wine cruet in the left hand. (If the priest is left-handed, this process may have to be reversed – experience will tell.) The lavabo follows: hold the basin in your left hand, have the towel over your left wrist, and pour water over the priest's fingers with the water cruet in your right hand. When placing the altar book stand on the altar, ensure that the book is open at the right page, and the stand at the right angle. All this should be done without hurry. When you arrive at the altar with anything, bow slightly to the priest before presenting it, and bow again before leaving the altar.

Acolytes' candles vary immensely in design, length and weight and, in fact, in every possible way. In processions, the candle should be carried in both hands. Ideally, the outer hand should be above the inner, but in practice it is best for each acolyte to carry his candle in the most comfortable fashion – within reason. A useful rule is to position the rim at the top of the candlestick level with the forehead; if the acolytes are of different heights, the taller one should position his candle thus, the shorter adjusting his candle to be level with that of his colleague. Acolytes should always take up or put down their candles together.

When not in use at the Eucharist, candles are normally placed near (or on) the credence table.

## Crucifer

The crucifer or cross-bearer carries the processional cross in processions. At the Eucharist it is not unusual for him to assist in other ways – for example, as a third acolyte at the Offertory, or as a book bearer. In some churches he wears an alb and tunicle (of the colour of the day) that is a reminder of the days when the sub-deacon of the Mass carried the cross in procession. The cross is carried in both hands, kept straight up and down and reasonably high. It should be high enough to prevent the foot of the staff rapping the carrier's shins in procession. When not in procession, the cross is placed in a stand, and is often used as the altar cross, especially with free-standing altars. In common with acolytes when carrying candles, the crucifer does not bow to the altar, or to anyone, when carrying the cross.

## Torch Bearers

Torch bearers are sometimes used at the consecration to add extra honour and dignity to the most solemn part of the Eucharist. The difference between a torch and an acolyte's candle used to be that the latter had a base, while the former did not, in order to convey a sense of impermanence. This is frequently not the case now, but the torch is usually of lighter construction. Torch bearers at the consecration should always be an even number – two, four, six, or eight (if an archbishop is celebrating); in practice, four is often the best number. If the bearers enter in pairs, the torch should be carried in the outside hand, and remain there if the bearers kneel. If they remain standing for the Eucharistic Prayer, it is preferable to hold the torches with both hands. Care should be taken that all torches are at the same height. The practice of raising the torches at points during the Eucharistic Prayer is all very well, but only if done all together and in a dignified manner. It must be practised beforehand. Torches are not normally carried in the entrance and retiring processions. They are, of course, carried in processions of the Blessed Sacrament, or when an image of Our Lord or Our Lady is carried in procession.

## Book Bearer

A book bearer is frequently required. When not in use the book is carried closed, in both hands, leaning against the chest. When the priest is reading from the book, hold it open with the fingers under the bottom and the thumbs behind it, keeping it upright; for obvious reasons, keep it still. The priest will adjust the height of the book, and he or the MC will turn the pages. It is helpful if the bearer is in place, with the book open at the correct page, at least a minute before the book is required.

## Banner Bearers

Banner bearers are sometimes required in processions. Banners vary in size – some are so large that they require men of prop-forward build to carry them – so care must be taken to allot a suitable bearer to each particular banner. Banners should be carried in a comfortable manner, not like a British Legion standard with elbows in the air. The use of small children as tassel boys is often more of a hindrance than a help, albeit popular with onlookers.

## Thurifer

With the exception of processions of the Blessed Sacrament, a procession is normally led by the thurifer with a smoking thurible. The thurible is normally carried in the outside hand, held by the disc or ring at the top, and should be swung enough to cause the emission of sweet-smelling smoke. Pyrotechnic displays, such as 'cartwheels' and 'figures-of-eight' are all very well, particularly in out-door processions, but should be kept to a minimum – they should always be to the glory of God, not of the thurifer! It is normal for the boat bearer (see p. 43.) to walk on the left, but if the thurifer is left-handed there is no earthly reason why the boat bearer should not walk on his right. When leading the procession, the thurifer should set a dignified pace, and must resist the temptation to speed up when faced with a long open aisle.

If the procession is accompanied by a hymn or hymns, the thurifer should check beforehand on the number of verses, so that he can, if necessary, adjust his speed accordingly.

If it is necessary to put more incense on the charcoal during a procession, this should be done 'on the move', without slowing the procession; the thurible is held open, and the boat bearer sprinkles incense on the charcoal.

In some churches, when the thurifer processes without his thurible (for example, at the Recession) it is customary for him to walk behind the crucifix and candles.

The great twentieth-century Roman Catholic liturgists, Fortescue and O'Connell (*The Ceremonies of the Roman Rite Described*, 10th ed., p. 43), say this:

> To handle a thurible neatly is a thing that requires some knowledge. This knowledge is acquired most easily by seeing the actions done by someone who already knows.

It is one of the many things, not really difficult or complicated, that requires many words to explain.

This is sound advice. It is doubtful if anyone ever learnt to handle a thurible solely from a textbook. It is much the best thing to find an experienced practitioner, and ask him to teach you. Someone once asked me, 'My church is just starting to use incense; I am a "rookie" thurifer, please teach me how to do it.' I was more than happy to do this.

A few basic principles may none the less be borne in mind. Always make sure that the charcoal is, literally, red-hot. Self-igniting charcoal can be lit over a taper or candle, but a gas-fired (Bunsen type) burner is better; a pair of tongs is essential. The charcoal must be hot in order to provide smoke when incense is sprinkled on it.

Before incense has been placed in it, the thurible is normally carried in the left hand, open to allow air to pass over the charcoal; when incense has been put on and blessed, the thurible is closed and carried and swung in the right hand. It is normally swung in the direction of the procession, to an angle of about 30 degrees either side of the vertical. When standing still, the thurifer swings it across his body.

When incense is being put on by the priest, the thurifer should open the thurible and hold it still at a convenient height for the priest; care should be taken that the priest does not have to manoeuvre the incense spoon round the chains. When the priest has blessed the incense, the thurible is closed and handed to the priest so that he can take the disc in his left hand and the chains just above the bowl in his right. (If the priest is left-handed, the situation is reversed.) If the thurible is handed to an intermediary (deacon or MC), it is best to hand it with the chains straight up and down. When taking the thurible from someone else, the thurifer should take it as it is given, and adjust his grip afterwards.

When censing (the term 'incensing' is now considered archaic) a person or object, the thurible should be held at eye level or just below; the left hand, holding the disc, should be against the chest, while the right hand holds the chains just above the bowl. Using only the right wrist, the bowl is swung towards the person or object concerned; the left hand is not moved, neither is the body. Although it is not obligatory, many thurifers like to allow the bowl to bounce back against the chains; if this is done the chains must be kept taut.

There are differing views on the number of swings due to any particular person or object, but the following list is a fair guide:

| | |
|---|---|
| Three trebles or doubles | the Blessed Sacrament; images of Our Lord |
| Three doubles | the celebrant or officiant, a bishop, the Book of Gospels; the altar cross; the Paschal candle; the body of a deceased person |
| Two doubles | images of Our Lady; priests in choir; liturgical deacons |
| One single | servers; choir; people. |

The gifts on the altar are censed in the form of a cross (formerly three circular swings).

A group of people, including concelebrants, is normally censed with the requisite number of swings, one to the centre, one to the left, and one to the right. Wherever possible, this form of censing should be used, rather than censing each priest, server etc. individually.

It is customary to bow to a person before and after censing him.

The thurifer should always remember that, because of his position, he is a very high-profile server, but despite that, he must avoid drawing attention to himself, difficult though that may be. Thorough training, and practice, is the only way of ensuring this.

## Boat Bearer

The boat bearer is frequently a youngster, just setting out on his serving career. In practice, they must be old enough to assimilate and remember basic instructions; about six or seven is the best minimum age. The incense boat should be carried in both hands, kept level, with the spoon pointing away from the bearer, so as not to get caught up in the cotta. It is helpful if the bearer opens the boat before presenting it. If the thurifer trusts the bearer to put incense on the charcoal, the bearer should sprinkle it without spilling it. Above all, the boat bearer must keep pace with his thurifer in procession, and know how to wheel.

## Bishop's Servers

Bishop's servers are also known as vimpas (or vimpae), so called after the scarf-type veil that they wear over the cotta, and through which they hold the crosier, mitre or book. These servers are the immediate attendants on the bishop, and although three are provided for in most liturgical books, in actual fact two will usually suffice, especially if there is a bishop's chaplain or a second MC who can deal with the crozier.

The **crozier bearer** carries or holds the crozier when the bishop is not using it; it is often placed in a stand when not in use for long periods. The bearer holds the crozier with the crook pointing backwards over him, and hands it to the bishop so that the crook is pointing outwards over the people. If handed to an intermediary (deacon, MC, etc.), the crook should face the recipient.

The **book bearer** holds the book before the bishop at the throne, and is usually responsible for placing it on, and removing it from, the altar. When not in use, the book is carried flat against the chest. The bearer should know when the book is required, without prompting, and at what page it should be open.

The **mitre bearer** holds the bishop's mitre when he is not wearing it. It should be held upright, with the front showing and the fanons (ribbons attached to the back) hanging down. If handed to a deacon or the MC, it can be passed in this way; if handed direct to the bishop, the bearer should turn it round and hand it flat to the bishop with the back of the mitre uppermost and the fanons folded back over it. The bishop can then easily put it on himself.

In procession, the three bearers walk immediately behind the bishop, the **book bearer** in the centre, the **mitre bearer** on his right, and the **crozier bearer** on his left.

At the throne, if space permits, the **mitre bearer** and **crozier bearer** stand to the right and left respectively of the deacons at the throne; the **book bearer** stands where he most conveniently can.

# 8

# Movement

The highest expression of praise for a serving team is 'we didn't see you' or 'we didn't realize you were there'. Bearing in mind that servers have a distinct job to do, either singly or together, and cannot avoid being in the congregation's eye, this is not easy to achieve, but it is possible with training and practice. This attitude or disposition was once described by a Royal Navy chaplain as being the midpoint between the Royal Marines on parade and the Peruvian navy on an evening ashore!

For centuries, serving at the altar was the prerogative of men and boys. In modern times, girls and women have become widely accepted as regular servers and are an integral part of many a serving team.

## Standing, Sitting and Kneeling

The server must always realize that he is just that – one who serves. He is not a principal (whatever flamboyant thurifers may think); he is there to serve the priest and, through him, Almighty God. For this reason servers must never draw attention to themselves, either deliberately or inadvertently; neither must they be obsequious in either their actions or piety. All this brings us to the question of how servers stand and move in the sanctuary. The overriding considerations must be reverence and dignity.

These basic guidelines should always be followed:

- Arrive in the sacristy at least 15 minutes before the service is due to begin. Always wear black shoes and dark socks – never white trainers or fluorescent socks!
- If you own your cassock/cotta or alb, make sure it is always clean and pressed; if you wear a 'common-user' vestment, bring any faults to the attention of the person responsible for them.
- Make sure that any items of which you are in charge – charcoal, cruets etc. – are in position well before the start of the service.
- Try to be quiet, at least for the few minutes before the service begins.

When standing, stand up straight, with hands together in prayer on the front of your chest or thereabouts, fingers horizontal; look straight in front of you, or at the priest; try not to fidget. If you are holding something in one hand, place your free hand flat on your chest. Remember that, these days, those in the sanctuary are usually much nearer to the congregation than in times past, and that any unnecessary movement can be distracting to people sitting at the front of the nave.

When sitting, sit up straight, with hands folded in your lap or flat on your knees.

When kneeling, again keep your back straight, except when bowing low, as for instance at Benediction. If you move from sitting to kneeling, don't slide off your chair into the ground, but stand first; the same applies, in reverse, if moving from kneeling to sitting.

In many churches, two or more servers frequently stand or sit together – for example, the acolytes and crucifer, or torch bearers. In cases such as these, it is essential that all stand, sit or kneel together; a nod from one of the servers is all that is required for timing. Remember to look like a team.

When turning, although it really doesn't matter whether

a single server turns to his right or to his left, a useful rule of thumb is to turn towards the altar. When two servers (for example, a pair of acolytes) are concerned, they should always turn inwards, towards each other. With three servers (say, acolytes and crucifer), the outer two turn inwards towards the one in the middle.

From time to time it is necessary for three servers (for example acolytes and crucifer) moving in line abreast to change formation into line ahead, or vice versa. If at all possible, this should be avoided on the move – the result-ant evolution often puts one in mind of line dancing! It is usually possible to remain in line abreast by wheeling into the new direction. If it is absolutely necessary to change into single file, then the three servers should stop, turn (left or right), and then proceed. When changing from single file to line abreast, taking as an example the acolytes with the crucifer between them moving from their place in the sanctuary to before the altar, the leading acolyte should know exactly where he is going to stop, and when he does so, he should wait for a second or two to give his col-leagues time to arrive in their positions, and then all turn together. If each server turns individually, it looks both ragged and undisciplined. Practice beforehand is essential.

On the question of knowing where to stop (or stand) there are any number of landmarks that can be used as markers in your church: a pillar; a particular tile forma-tion in the floor; a candle; any number of items in and around the Sanctuary; and so on.

It is often necessary to remember that the shortest dis-tance between two points is a straight line. Square corners and right-angled turns are all very well, but can look man-nered and ponderous. For instance, when proceeding from the sanctuary step to the altar step, the direct (diagonal) route is often more appropriate and dignified, using, as it were, the hypotenuse of a triangle rather than its other two sides.

Bowing to the altar, the cross or the priest is an inclination of the head and shoulders; a profound bow involves bending from the waist, but not doubling up completely, which is most undignified. Custom varies from church to church. It is not normal to bow to the altar when passing it in procession.

Genuflecting involves bending *one* knee until it touches the floor, and then straightening up; the back should be kept straight. One should always genuflect to the tabernacle and to the Blessed Sacrament as an extra sign of devotion to Our Lord's actual presence. If the tabernacle is in the sanctuary it is usual to genuflect to it on first arrival and on finally leaving, but here again practice does vary, as it does over the question of whether or not to genuflect to the consecrated Sacrament on the altar during the Eucharist. The practice of genuflecting to a bishop before presenting something to him is now virtually extinct.

## Mistakes

Even in the best-regulated circles mistakes can occur. If you realize that you have made an error, don't stop and look confused, but carry on as if nothing has happened, bow solemnly to the altar or the celebrant, and quietly return to your place. The chances are that no one will notice. Don't worry about it – just concentrate on getting the next movement right.

## Processions

Processions can be a most impressive part of ceremonial, or can resemble a rabble leaving a football match. Those leading should set a reasonable, dignified pace – neither a rush nor a funereal crawl; those following should take their pace

from those ahead of them, maintaining a sensible gap
(usually about five or six feet) from those immediately
ahead. If you are walking two, three or four abreast,
always maintain a straight line with your colleagues,
particularly on corners, where the inside server steps short;
this is particularly important in the case of acolytes and
crucifer. (Where there is insufficient room for three to walk
abreast, remember that the acolytes lead the crucifer.)
Chapter 9 has details of the order of processions.

# Step by Step

## Said Celebration

Traditions vary nowadays as to whether or not the server robes for a said celebration of the Eucharist. If you do, you need to be present in the sacristy at least five minutes before the service begins. That means you will already have checked that all is ready for the service.

You need to check the following:
- The cruets, bread box, lavabo bowl and towel, and the chalice, paten, pall and corporal, are on the credence table. (If there are likely to be more than a dozen or so communicants you may need a small ciborium as well.)
- The altar book is on its stand on the altar in the centre if the priest takes the whole of the service at the altar, or on the priest's left side if he goes there at the Offertory.
- If the priest takes the Liturgy of the Word at a separate place, a *legilium* or lectern, the book with the readings and the text of the Eucharist is there and ready.

The priest may ask you to read the lesson and lead the responsorial psalm, so make sure you have looked at them in advance and that your copy of the readings is where you expect it to be!

If you are robed, lead the priest from the sacristy to the chapel just before the time of the service. It may be the custom for you to ring the sacristy bell to announce the service is about to begin, and some churches have a small bowl of holy water near the sacristy door so that you and the priest can make the sign of the cross with it as you enter the church. If you pass the high altar it is the custom to bow to the altar. If the high altar has the reserved Sacrament there, or if you pass a chapel where the Sacrament is reserved, you should genuflect or bow profoundly according to your church's custom. If the priest does not expect you to robe, go to the chapel and wait for the service to begin.

Join in the service with everyone else, taking a lead in the spoken responses. Read your lesson and lead the psalm if you are expected to do so, and listen carefully to the words of the Holy Gospel. Exchange the peace with the congregation.

At the Offertory come to the credence table. Hand the priest the chalice and paten, with the pall and corporal. The priest will spread the corporal unless you have already been asked to do so. Make sure you already know how many people are in the congregation so that you can tell the priest when you present the bread box. Then present the wine and water as described in Chapter 7. The priest may say the Offertory prayers, to which the confident response is 'Blessed be God for ever!' Then wash the priest's fingers, again as described in Chapter 7. Place everything back on the credence table and return to your seat.

Lead the responses at the beginning of the Eucharistic prayer, the Sursum Corda, and listen carefully to the prayer. In some churches the server rings a bell or a gong after the words of Jesus, 'Do this in remembrance of me', or at the end of the prayer. Receive Communion and be on hand for the ablutions, the ritual cleansing of the chalice and paten.

The ablutions used to be quite complicated. Nowadays you need only offer the water, pouring a little in the chalice and, if required, on the paten. The priest may ask you to pour a little water over his fingers to cleanse them. Receive back the chalice and paten, with the refolded corporal and pall, from the priest and place them on the credence. At the end of the service lead the priest back to the sacristy if you are robed, or wait until all have finished their private prayers and return all that is on the credence to the sacristy.

## Sung Celebration

Most of the occasions on which you serve will be at the Sunday main Eucharist. There may be a team of up to four servers for this service, a crucifer, acolytes, and a book bearer or master of ceremonies (MC). The way in which the ceremonial is devised will suit your location, the church in which you worship. Your church may be round, square, rectangular or cruciform. It may be Norman, Early English, Classical or modern. So what goes on in the church will be determined by its shape, its architecture and its furnishings.

Table 1 describes what is likely to take place at each main point in the service. It is in tabular form so that you can see how what you do relates to the other servers and to the celebrant and deacon.

Table 1: The main points of the service

| Celebrant | Deacon | Crucifer and acolytes | MC/Book bearer |
|---|---|---|---|
| **Entrance Procession**<br><br>During the *Entrance Hymn* follow the servers and deacon to the altar. Bow with the deacon and go to the president's chair. | **Entrance Procession**<br><br>During the *Entrance Hymn* follow the servers to the altar. Bow with the celebrant and place the Gospel Book on the altar. Go to the deacon's seat on the right of the celebrant. | **Entrance Procession**<br><br>During the *Entrance Hymn* crucifer, acolytes and MC/book bearer lead the deacon and the celebrant to the altar. | |
| Greet the people and lead the *Collect for Purity* etc. Absolve the people. The president introduces a period of silent prayer with the words 'Let us pray' or a more specific bidding. | Remain standing. The deacon may introduce the Confession. | Remain by your seats. | MC brings the altar book to the celebrant's chair for the *Greeting and Collect for Purity, Confession, Kyrie/Gloria* and the *Collect of the Day* and stands before the celebrant. |
| Sit for the *Readings*. | Sit for the *Readings*. | Sit for the *Readings*. | Sit for the *Readings*. |

| Celebrant | Deacon | Crucifer and acolytes | MC/Book bearer |
|---|---|---|---|
| **Gospel Procession** | **Gospel Procession** | **Gospel Procession** | **Gospel Procession** |
| Remain seated. The celebrant may bless the deacon. Stand for the *Gospel*. | Ask the celebrant for a blessing and collect the Book of the Gospels from the altar; then, bowing to the altar, follow the crucifer and acolytes to a place in the midst of the congregation or to the lectern. Announce the Gospel. At the end the Book of the Gospels is raised; the deacon stands aside and follows the crucifer and acolytes back to the crossing. He puts the Book of the Gospels on the altar or in another suitable place. | During the *Alleluia Chant/Gradual Hymn* crucifer and acolytes come out for the Gospel Procession and lead the deacon and book bearer to a place in the midst of the congregation or to the lectern. Acolytes turn inwards and the book bearer stands between them facing east, or they stand either side of the lectern. Return in the same way. | During the *Alleluia Chant/Gradual Hymn* come out for the Gospel Procession and lead the deacon to a place in the midst of the congregation. (If the Gospel is read from the lectern you might not be needed.) Stand between the acolytes, facing east. The deacon may leave the Book of the Gospels with the book bearer, who puts it in a suitable place. |

| | | | |
|---|---|---|---|
| Preach, or sit for, the *Sermon*. | Preach, or sit for, the *Sermon*. | Sit for the *Sermon*. | Sit for the *Sermon*. |
| Stand for the *Creed*. | Stand for the *Creed*. | Stand for the *Creed*. | Stand for the *Creed*. |
| Conclude the *Intercessions* with the Collect or 'Merciful Father . . .' | Remain standing for the *Intercessions*. The deacon may lead the petitions. | Remain standing for the *Intercessions*. | The book bearer brings the altar book to the chair for the Collect at the end of the *Intercessions* and remains for the *Peace*. |
| Announce the *Peace*. Share the *Peace* with the sanctuary party and with the congregation. | After the celebrant has said 'The peace of the Lord be always with you' and received the reply say: 'Let us offer one another a sign of peace.' Share the *Peace* with the sanctuary party and with the congregation. | Share the *Peace* with the sanctuary party. | Share the *Peace* with the sanctuary party. |

| Celebrant | Deacon | Crucifer and acolytes | MC/Book bearer |
|---|---|---|---|
| **Offertory Procession** | **Offertory Procession** | **Offertory Procession** | **Offertory Procession** |
| Wait at the chair until the deacon indicates that all is prepared. Go to the altar and receive the paten and chalice from the deacon. Say the *Offertory prayers* quietly. Receive the lavabo. Bless the collection. | Receive from the servers the ciborium, chalices and paten. Charge the chalices, add water and hand the paten and then the chalice to the celebrant for the *Offertory prayers*.<br><br>Step back while the celebrant receives the lavabo. Then remain at his right side. | The acolytes assist with the preparation of the altar, bringing the chalice and paten to the deacon/celebrant, and offering the lavabo to the celebrant.<br><br>The crucifer receives the collection in the bowl, and faces the celebrant, who blesses it. It is then set aside. | The book bearer places the altar book on the altar. |
| Declaim the *Eucharistic Prayer* as customary. At the *Doxology* of the prayer, elevate the Host. The deacon elevates the chalice. | At the *Doxology* of the *Eucharistic Prayer* elevate the chalice when the celebrant elevates the Host. | Stand throughout the *Eucharistic Prayer*. | Stand throughout the *Eucharistic Prayer*. |
| Say the *Lord's Prayer* (with hands extended). | Say the *Lord's Prayer* (with hands joined). | Remain standing for the *Lord's Prayer*. | Remain standing for the *Lord's Prayer*. |

| Holy Communion | Holy Communion | Holy Communion | Holy Communion |
|---|---|---|---|
| Receive Communion, then communicate the deacon, the servers and the people.<br><br>At the end of the distribution the deacon performs the ablutions at the altar or at the credence table or in another suitable place. In the absence of a deacon the celebrant or other authorized person does this. | The deacon receives Communion and then follows the celebrant to communicate to the servers and then the congregation.<br><br>At the end of the distribution supervise the ablutions, then return to your chair. | After receiving Holy Communion sit or kneel. Assist with the ablutions, pouring water into the vessels. | After receiving Holy Communion sit or kneel. The book bearer may tidy the altar, folding the corporal and removing the altar book. |

| Celebrant | Deacon | Crucifer and acolytes | MC/Book bearer |
|---|---|---|---|
| **After Communion** | **After Communion** | **After Communion** | **After Communion** |
| Say the *Post-communion Prayer*. | | Stand for the *Post-communion Prayer*. | Stand for the *Post-communion Prayer*. |
| Bless the people. Do not say the *Dismissal* if there is a deacon! | Say/sing the *Dismissal* adding 'Alleluia, alleluia!' in Eastertide. | Remain standing for the *Blessing and Dismissal*. | Remain standing for the *Blessing and Dismissal*. |
| **Exit Procession** | **Exit Procession** | **Exit Procession** | **Exit Procession** |
| Come to the altar, kiss the altar or bow from behind with the deacon. Walk with the deacon procession. | Come to the altar, kiss the altar or bow from behind with the celebrant. Walk on the celebrant's right in the procession. | Crucifer and acolytes come out for the procession and lead the book bearer, deacon and celebrant to the sacristy. | Come out for the procession and follow the crucifer and acolytes to the sacristy. |

## Solemn Celebration

The word 'solemn' in this context does not mean lugubri-
ous or killjoy! It means that things are done with as much
dignity as possible and the ceremonial may be more elaborate. Churches that use incense weekly or at festivals will
do so at a Solemn Eucharist.

Table 2 shows the likely movements of the servers at a
Solemn Eucharist where incense is used.

**Table 2: Ceremonial of the servers when incense is used**

| Crucifer and acolytes | MC/Book bearer | Thurifer |
|---|---|---|
| **Entrance Procession**<br><br>During the *Entrance Hymn* crucifer, acolytes and MC/book bearer lead the deacon and the celebrant to the altar. | | **Entrance Procession**<br><br>During the *Entrance Hymn* the thurifer comes to the celebrant, who puts incense on and blesses it. The thurifer comes to the head of the procession and leads the crucifer, acolytes and MC/book bearer, deacon and celebrant to the altar. At the altar, after the celebrant has reverenced, the thurifer hands the censer to the celebrant, who censes the altar. The thurifer receives back the censer and retires to his place or to the sacristy. |

## Table 2: Continued

| Crucifer and acolytes | MC/Book bearer | Thurifer |
|---|---|---|
| **Gospel Procession**<br><br>During the *Alleluia Chant/Gradual Hymn* crucifer and acolytes come out for the procession and lead the deacon and book bearer to a place in the midst of the congregation or to the lectern. Acolytes turn inwards and the book bearer stands between them facing east, or acolytes stand either side of the lectern.<br>　Return in the same way. | **Gospel Procession**<br><br>During the *Alleluia Chant/Gradual Hymn* come out for the procession and lead the deacon to a place in the midst of the congregation. (If the Gospel is read from the lectern you might not be needed.) Acolytes turn inwards and the book bearer stands between them facing east. The deacon may leave the Book of the Gospels with the book bearer, who puts it in a suitable place. | **Gospel Procession**<br><br>During the *Alleluia Chant/Gradual Hymn* come out for the procession. Go to the celebrant, who will put incense on and bless it. Lead the servers and the deacon or celebrant to a place in the midst of the congregation or to the lectern. Stand close to the person reading the Gospel who, after it has been announced, will receive the censer and cense the Book of the Gospels. Swing the censer gently as the Gospel is read and then lead the procession back to the sanctuary. |
| **Offertory Procession**<br><br>The acolytes assist with the prepara-tion of the altar: bringing the chalice | **Offertory Procession**<br><br>The book bearer places the altar book on the altar. | **Offertory Procession**<br><br>After the altar has been prepared (or during this prepara-tion if there is a |

## Table 2: Continued

| Crucifer and acolytes | MC/Book bearer | Thurifer |
|---|---|---|
| and paten to the deacon/celebrant; offering the lavabo to the celebrant. The crucifer receives the collection in the bowl, and faces the celebrant, who blesses it. It is then set aside. | | deacon) go to the celebrant, who will put incense on the charcoal and bless it. Move to the altar. After the celebrant has said the *Offertory Prayers* present the censer. The celebrant censes the gifts and the altar. Receive back the censer and cense the celebrant, the deacon, the other servers and the congregation. |
| Stand throughout the *Eucharistic Prayer*. | Stand throughout the *Eucharistic Prayer*. | Stand throughout the *Eucharistic Prayer*, gently swinging the censer. You may add incense during the *Benedictus* or ask the boat bearer or MC to do so. It does not need to be blessed. Cense the Host and the chalice if they are elevated. |
| Remain standing for the *Lord's Prayer*. | Remain standing for the *Lord's Prayer*. | It may be appropriate for you to leave the Sanctuary at the *Lord's Prayer* returning immediately |

## Table 2: Continued

| Crucifer and acolytes | MC/Book bearer | Thurifer |
|---|---|---|
|  |  | without the censer, or to put the censer on its stand and remain standing. |
| **Holy Communion**<br><br>After receiving Holy Communion sit or kneel. Assist with the ablutions, pouring water into the vessels. | **Holy Communion**<br><br>After receiving Holy Communion sit or kneel. The book bearer may tidy the altar, folding the corporal and removing the altar book. | **Holy Communion**<br><br>After receiving Holy Communion sit or kneel. |
| **After Communion**<br><br>Stand for the *Post-communion Prayer* and *Blessing*. | **After Communion**<br><br>Stand for the *Post-communion Prayer* and *Blessing*. | **After Communion**<br><br>Stand for the *Post-communion Prayer* and *Blessing*. |
| **Exit Procession**<br><br>Crucifer and acolytes come out for the procession and lead the book bearer, deacon and celebrant to the sacristy. | **Exit Procession**<br><br>Crucifer and acolytes come out for the procession and lead the book bearer, deacon and celebrant to the sacristy. | **Exit Procession**<br><br>While it is not strictly correct you may lead the procession with the thurible, or, better, walk behind the acolytes without it. |

## Benediction

Benediction is a service constructed round the action of blessing the people with the exposed Blessed Sacrament. It can stand on its own as a service, or may follow the Eucharist (where it takes the place of the Blessing), Evensong or Vespers.

The priest (or bishop) normally wears a white cope; he may be assisted by two other priests in copes, or by one or two deacons in dalmatics.

The Blessed Sacrament may be brought to the altar in solemn procession (as on the Feast of Corpus Christi – see Chapter 6), or placed thereon by the deacon, in which case all should be in position, before the Sacrament is brought in (see Figure 1). The monstrance should be placed on a corporal. In some churches it is the custom to remove the altar cross, but this is not really necessary, particularly if the cross stands behind, rather than on, the altar. As a general rule, if the tabernacle from which the Blessed Sacrament is brought is outside the sanctuary, the deacon should use the humeral veil when carrying it.

**Figure 1: Positions for Benediction**

| Altar |

| Ac | D Pr D | Ac |
| Th | MC | Th* |

*when second thurifer is present

Servers should take care to keep as still as possible when kneeling.

Acolytes place their candles on the step in front of them; all kneel as the monstrance is placed on the altar. Priest and deacons, MC and thurifer stand, incense is put on,[1] all kneel again and the Blessed Sacrament is censed by the priest. If no deacons are present, MC and thurifer kneel either side of the priest and hold up the cope. The hymn 'O salutaris hostia' is often sung at this point.

There follow intercessions and/or prayers led by the priest, sometimes including a reading or a hymn. All remain kneeling; the thurible is swung gently.

At the end of the prayers etc., the hymn 'Tantum ergo' is sung; all bow low at the first line, and remain bowing until the priest rises. The deacons, MC and thurifer rise with him, incense is again put on, all kneel and the priest censes the Blessed Sacrament. After censing, it is usually more dignified for the MC alone to rise and take the thurible from the priest and return it to the thurifer.

The priest *alone* then stands, and sings a versicle/ response and the Collect. The MC collects the humeral veil and places it round the priest's shoulders. The MC kneels, the deacons stand and the priest and deacons go up to the top step, where the priest takes up the monstrance, the deacons kneel, and the priest blesses the people, making the sign of the cross with the monstrance. The bell is rung three times by the MC (or an acolyte). The priest then replaces the monstrance on the altar and the priest and deacons return to the bottom step.

The MC takes the humeral veil and a further prayer or meditation follows, followed by an antiphon (or Psalm

---

1 Modern Roman Catholic practice is for the priest to bless the incense at this point, and when it is put on again during Tantum ergo. However, in many churches it is not the custom to bless incense in front of the exposed Sacrament.

117), during which a deacon removes the monstrance, returning the Blessed Sacrament to the tabernacle. The bell is rung as the Sacrament leaves the altar.

All then rise and go out, the thurifer(s) leading.


## Processions

Processions have formed an integral part of Catholic worship for centuries. The medieval English church was famous for its processions, which were sometimes led by two or even three crosses, and constructed strictly on the basis of formal rank. This love of formal processions survives today in the great British state occasions.

Broadly speaking, processions fall into two types: those which are simply a means of getting a large body of people from A to B in good order, and those which have a liturgical, theological or historical significance. The Entrance Procession at the Eucharist is an example of the first type; the Procession of Palms on Palm Sunday, or a Corpus Christi Procession of the Blessed Sacrament fall into the second category. The great outdoor processions often seen at Pilgrimages and the like can fall into either category, or be an amalgam of both.

The various types of processions are described in the following notes. These notes should be read in conjunction with Chapters 6 and 8. Priests (if available) in choir dress replace concelebrants if the Eucharist is not concelebrated.

The following abbreviations are used in the boxed text below.

| Ac | acolyte | C | celebrant | Mb | mitre bearer |
|----|---------|---|-----------|----|----|
| Bb | boat bearer | Cc | concelebrant | MC | master of ceremonies |
| Bk | book bearer | Cr | crucifer | Tch | torch bearer |
| Bp | bishop | D | deacon | Th | thurifer |

## 1a. Entrance Procession

The Entrance Procession may be said to set the tone of the service; if it is dignified and smart, it can be assumed that the ceremonial will be likewise. The diagram assumes the availability of two priest concelebrants and a deacon. The deacon carries the Book of Gospels: the MC may carry the president's book. Incense is put on at the church door. A banner would be carried before or after the choir. The Retiring Procession is in the same order, except that the deacon walks alongside or in front of the celebrant, and the thurifer follows the cross and candles.

```
        ↑

     Bb  Th
   Ac  Cr  Ac
    Tch  Tch
      Choir
       MC
        D
      Cc  Cc
        C
```

## 1b. Entrance Procession – bishop presiding

This form of procession is used when the diocesan or area bishop celebrates the Eucharist in a church building or at a function. A crozier bearer is not considered necessary; in practice the MC walks immediately ahead of the bishop. The book bearer carries the president's book.

```
        ↑

     Bb  Th
   Ac  Cr  Ac
    Tch  Tch
      Choir
        D
      Cc  Cc
        Cc
       MC
     D  Bp  D
     Bk    Mb
```

## 2. Gospel Procession at the Eucharist

The Holy Gospel, being the Word of Our Lord, is accorded a greater degree of honour and ceremony than any other reading at the Eucharist. Incense and lights are used at its proclamation. Opinions (and authorities) differ as to whether or not the processional crucifix is appropriate to the Gospel Procession as, with the book, it presents two images of the Word. Generally speaking, the crucifix may be considered appropriate if a procession outside the sanctuary precedes the proclamation of the Gospel. Space restrictions sometimes make it difficult to 'turn the procession round' after the Gospel; if so, it is in order for the cross and candles, rather than the thurifer, to lead the procession back to the sanctuary.

↑

Bb   Th

Ac   Cr   Ac

Bk

MC

D

## 3. Christmas – Midnight Mass

Either the Entrance or the Retiring Procession may make a station at the crib in order to bless it and to place the Christ child in it. If holy water is used, a torch bearer can carry the container. It is best if the deacon does not carry the Book of Gospels – it can be placed on the altar before the service. Great care must be taken to get servers into suitable positions before the crib, bearing in mind that the thurifer will have to present the thurible to the celebrant, and that the procession must re-form with the minimum of fuss after the blessing of the crib. How exactly this is done is usually dictated by the space available.

## 4. Epiphany

The Wise Men's gifts of gold, frankincense and myrrh are often presented by young (but not too young!) children during the Eucharist. They can be brought in as part of the Entrance Procession, in which case the bearers follow the cross and candles, or they can form part of the Offertory Procession, which in some churches is preceded by lights. In either case, the MC or servers must be on hand to place the gifts on or near the altar, as directed. Another, highly descriptive way of emphasizing the Epiphany is for the figures of the three Wise Men to be carried in the Entrance Procession, preferably by young people, possibly vested, representing the last part of their journey. Again, the bearers follow the cross and candles. As at Midnight Mass, a station is made at the crib and the Magi are placed in the crib (the shepherds having gone their way, rejoicing) and blessed by the celebrant. By closely following the liturgical pattern set at Christmas, this helps to emphasize the importance of Epiphany.

## 5. The Presentation of Christ in the Temple (Candlemas)

The Procession of Light normally takes place before the Eucharist. Handheld candles are blessed and lit in a convenient place outside the church, and all who are able, priests, servers and people, carry these candles into the church in procession. The order is as for the Entrance Procession, with the people following the celebrant. The Book of Gospels is placed on the altar before the service.

If the Candlemas ceremonies take place at the end of the Eucharist, the candles are blessed in the sanctuary, distributed and lit, and the people follow the Retiring Procession (thurifer leading) out of the church.

## 6. Palm Sunday

The spectacular Procession of Palms should ideally be out of doors, in order closely to re-enact Our Lord's triumphant entry into Jerusalem. All who can carry palm branches do so, and it is usual for the people, carrying palm crosses, to follow the celebrant into the church. The order is basically the same as for the Entrance Procession. It may, however, be advantageous to split the choir, placing part of it amongst the people, in order to support the congregational singing.

## 7. Maundy (or Holy) Thursday

The Eucharist – the Liturgy of the Last Supper – ends with a solemn procession from the main altar to the altar of repose (usually in a side chapel), re-enacting Our Lord's journey after the Last Supper to Gethsemane. The celebrant carries the Blessed Sacrament, Our Lord's body, in the form of consecrated hosts in a ciborium, covered with the humeral veil. The ciborium is placed on the altar of repose, surrounded by lights, and silent watch is kept before it at least until midnight, the time of Our Lord's arrest. The cross is not normally used; the two thurifers should carry their thuribles in the inside hand, on a short chain.

The Hosts are used for communion at the Good Friday Liturgy (see the discussion of Corpus Christi in Chapter 6).

```
            ↑

       Ac   Ac
       Bb   MC
       Cc   Cc
       Th   Th
      D*  C  D*
      Tch   Tch
```

*If no deacons are present, Ccs may flank the C.

## 8. Good Friday

The Liturgy of Our Lord's passion and death is a service of such power and intensity – and beauty – as to leave the participants emotionally exhausted. Servers are completely exposed and have a great responsibility – all must be done with solemnity, reverence and dignity. The minimum number of servers (MC + 2) is used; in some churches four acolytes are used, splitting the duties between the two pairs. The veiled crucifix is carried in by the deacon, and is usually unveiled at three pre-determined stations; it is then set up for the Veneration. Acolytes carry candles; they genuflect at each unveiling, and stand either side of the cross during the Veneration. The cross is finally placed on or behind the altar, with the candles either side. If there is insufficient room, acolytes precede the cross. The MC sets a slow pace; the procession may be accompanied by a suitable hymn, or take place in complete silence.

The Blessed Sacrament, in the ciborium, is brought from the altar of repose in procession, prior to being distributed. Acolytes carry candles (not those carried with the cross), and the deacon wears the humeral veil. The procession may follow the same route as the cross, and may either be accompanied by a hymn or take place in complete silence. Acolytes place their candles near those already in position. The Retiring Procession is in the same order as the Entrance, unless the church adheres to the old custom of the service breaking up in disorder.

**Entrance Procession**

↑

Ac   Ac
( Ac)   (Ac )
MC
D
C

**Procession of the Cross**

↑

MC
Ac   D   Ac

**Procession of the Blessed Sacrament**

↑

MC
Ac   D   Ac

## 9. Holy Saturday

The Easter Vigil, which may begin after dark on Holy Saturday, is a spectacular, indeed theatrical, service, which heralds the most joyful time in the Church's year – the resurrection. After being blessed at the New Fire, the great Paschal candle is carried into the church in solemn procession by the deacon, followed by the servers, priests and people. Incense is put on coals from the New Fire at the start of the procession; priests' and servers' hand candles, and the acolytes' candles, are lit at one of the Lumen Christi stations. Torchbearers may be used for lighting these candles. The candle is placed in its stand, preferably in the middle of the sanctuary, and censed before the singing of the Exultet.

Following the Gospel (in some churches, acolytes do not carry candles) or the homily, the priest and servers go to the font for the blessing of the water and the renewal of baptismal vows, and for baptisms, if any. The procession is led by the deacon with the Paschal candle and all carry unlit hand candles or tapers. All hand candles are lit from the Paschal candle. The procession returns to the altar in the same order.

The service continues with the Peace and the Offertory – and the first Eucharist of Easter.

**N.B.** In all Holy Week processions (items 6–9), if torch bearers are not available a second MC may be used. It is preferable that the MC should always be as near as possible to the celebrant; the MC should also know exactly every detail of the liturgy, and everybody's part in it. Rehearsals are absolutely essential; shoddy, unrehearsed ceremonial is distracting to the people, and more importantly, disrespectful to Almighty God.

**Procession of the New Light**

↑

D
Bb Th
Ac Ac
Tch Tch
Choir
Cc Cc
MC
C
People

**Procession to the Font**

↑

D
Bb Th
Ac Ac
Tch Tch
Cc Cc
MC
C

## 10. Easter Day, Ascension Day, Pentecost, Christ the King

These four great festivals are suitably marked by processions. In practice, the Entrance Procession is usually expanded into a grand procession with banners, which may be placed before and behind the choir, and which may go all round the church before arriving in the sanctuary; the celebrant may wear a cope. If the weather is suitable, particularly at Easter, the processional route may go outside and enter the church by the main door. In some churches it is the custom to use a second thurifer, and perhaps two torch bearers immediately ahead of the priests and deacons.

The Retiring Procession should be as usual, without banners.

These festivals, especially Easter, are occasions of great joy and exuberance, but dignity should always be the overriding factor.

## 11. Corpus Christi

A solemn Procession of the Blessed Sacrament is often part of the Corpus Christi Eucharist, and can be appropriate on other occasions (such as Maundy Thursday). The consecrated host is carried in a monstrance, held high by the celebrant or priest, who wears the humeral veil and a cope. If the procession goes out of doors, a canopy can be carried over the Blessed Sacrament, but only the celebrant and deacons should actually be under it. Thurifers should swing thuribles on a short chain in the inside hand. If there is insufficient room, two torch bearers should walk ahead of the thurifers and two following the Sacrament. The MC carries the hand bells, ringing them at regular intervals. The pace should be slow and dignified.

```
              ↑

         Ac  Cr  Ac
             Bb
           Cc  Cc
      Tch    MC    Tch
           Th   Th
      Tch D* C D* Tch
         Tch      Tch
```

*If deacons are not available, concelebrants in copes may flank the celebrant.

STEP BY STEP 73

---

**12. Procession of the Blessed Virgin Mary (BVM)**
On feasts of Our Lady, an image of the Blessed Virgin is sometimes carried in procession, either in the Entrance Procession or at another time during the service.

↑

Bb  Th

Ac  Cr  Ac

Tch        Tch

Image of BVM

Tch        Tch

MC

Cc    Cc

D

C

---

## Funerals

The funeral service for one of the faithful frequently takes the form of a Requiem Mass, when, in the context of the Eucharist, the soul of the deceased is sped on its way, supported by the prayers of the remaining faithful.

The ceremonial of the Eucharist itself varies little, if at all, from a normal Eucharist, but the service may end with the Solemn Commendation, which may be carried out by the celebrant of the Eucharist or by another priest. If carried out by the celebrant he may remain in the chasuble or wear a cope the colour of the Eucharist (purple, black or white); another priest would normally wear a cope. The coffin is on a catafalque in the chancel or at the head of the nave.

A pall may cover the coffin; and flowers, a cross and a title, or other symbols of the life and faith of the deceased person, are placed on or near it. Before the Commendation and Farewell anything placed on the coffin is removed by servers. Two experienced servers, who fold the pall ends-to-middle from either end, now remove the pall and set it to one side.

The priest may address the people and say appropriate prayers or a reading over the coffin. He then puts on and blesses incense. He takes the holy water and walks round the coffin, asperging (sprinkling) it; he then takes the thurible and walks round the coffin again, censing it; the MC may lead him on both occasions. This may be done in silence, to musical accompaniment or to the recital of the Lord's Prayer.

The priest than says the words of the Commendation, the pall bearers approach and lift and turn the coffin, and the procession goes out of the church, thurifer and cross and candles leading and the priest immediately ahead of the coffin. It is usual for family mourners to follow the coffin. The thurifer may cense the coffin (three doubles) as it is put into the hearse or grave. All must be done slowly and with dignity, particularly when the coffin is being lifted and the thurifer is taking his place at the head of the procession.

# 10

# An Order for Night Prayer (Compline)

*Note*

The ancient office of Compline derives its name from a Latin word meaning 'completion' (*completorium*). It is above all a service of quietness and reflection before rest at the end of the day. It is most effective when the ending is indeed an ending, without additions, conversation or noise. If there is business to be done, it should come first. If the service is in church, those present depart in silence. if at home, they go quietly to bed.

## Preparation

The Lord almighty grant us a quiet night and a perfect end.
**Amen.**

Our help is in the name of the Lord
**who made heaven and earth.**

*A period of silence for reflection on the past day follows.*

Most merciful God,
I confess to you,
before the whole company of heaven and one another,
that I have sinned in thought, word and deed
and in what I have failed to do.
Forgive me my sins,
heal me by your Spirit
and raise me to new life in Christ. Amen.

O God, make speed to save us.
O Lord, make haste to help us.

Glory to the Father and to the Son
and to the Holy Spirit;
as it was in the beginning is now
and shall be for ever. Amen.
Alleluia.

*The following hymn is said or sung.*

Before the ending of the day,
Creator of the world, we pray
That you, with steadfast love, would keep
Your watch around us while we sleep.

From evil dreams defend our sight,
From fears and terrors of the night;
Tread underfoot our deadly foe
That we no sinful thought may know.

O Father, that we ask be done
Through Jesus Christ, your only Son;
And Holy Spirit, by whose breath
Our souls are raised to life from death.

## The Word of God

Psalmody

Psalm 134

1   Come, bless the Lord, all you servants of the Lord, *
    you that by night stand in the house of the Lord.

2   Lift up your hands towards the sanctuary *
    and bless the Lord.

3   The Lord who made heaven and earth *
    give you blessing out of Zion.

Glory to the Father and to the Son
and to the Holy Spirit;
as it was in the beginning is now
and shall be for ever. Amen.

Scripture Reading

*One of the following short lessons or another suitable passage is read*

You, O Lord, are in the midst of us and we are called by
your name; leave us not, O Lord our God.     *Jeremiah 14.9*

*(or)*

Be sober, be vigilant, because your adversary the devil is
prowling round like a roaring lion, seeking for someone to
devour. Resist him, strong in the faith.     *1 Peter 5.8–9*

*(or)*

The servants of the Lamb shall see the face of God, whose name will be on their foreheads. There will be no more night: they will not need the light of a lamp or the light of the sun, for God will be their light, and they will reign for ever and ever.     *Revelation 22.4–5*

*The following responsory may be said*

Into your hands, O Lord, I commend my spirit.
**Into your hands, O Lord, I commend my spirit.**
For you have redeemed me, Lord God of truth.
**I commend my spirit.**
Glory to the Father, and to the Son, and to the Holy Spirit.
**Into your hands, O Lord, I commend my spirit.**

*Or, in Easter*

Into your hands, O Lord, I commend my spirit. Alleluia, alleluia.
**Into your hands, O Lord, I commend my spirit. Alleluia, alleluia.**
For you have redeemed me, Lord God of truth.
**I commend my spirit. Alleluia, alleluia.**
Glory to the Father, and to the Son, and to the Holy Spirit.
**Into your hands, O Lord, I commend my spirit. Alleluia, alleluia.**

Keep me as the apple of your eye.
**Hide me under the shadow of your wings.**

## Gospel Canticle

*The Nunc dimittis (The Song of Simeon) is said or sung*

**Save us, O Lord, while waking,**
**and guard us while sleeping,**
**that awake we may watch with Christ**
**and asleep may rest in peace.**

1    Now, Lord, you let your servant go in peace: *
    your word has been fulfilled.

2    My own eyes have seen the salvation *
    which you have prepared in the sight of every people;

3    A light to reveal you to the nations *
    and the glory of your people Israel.      *Luke 2.29–32*

Glory to the Father and to the Son
and to the Holy Spirit;
as it was in the beginning is now
and shall be for ever. Amen.

**Save us, O Lord, while waking,**
**and guard us while sleeping,**
**that awake we may watch with Christ**
**and asleep may rest in peace.**

## Prayers

Visit this place, O Lord, we pray,
and drive far from it the snares of the enemy;
may your holy angels dwell with us and guard us in peace,
and may your blessing be always upon us;
through Jesus Christ our Lord.
**Amen.**

Almighty and everlasting God, I approach the sacrament of
your Only-begotten Son, our Lord Jesus Christ. I come to it

as one who is sick to the physician who will save my life, as unclean to the fountain of mercy, as blind to the radiance of eternal light, as poor and needy to the Lord of heaven and earth; praying that in your boundless generosity you will deign to cure my sickness, wash my sins away, enlighten my blindness, enrich my poverty and clothe my nakedness.

May I receive the Bread of Angels, the King of Kings and Lord of Lords, with such humble reverence and devout contrition, such faith and purity, and such good resolutions as may help my salvation. Grant me grace to receive not only the sacrament of the Lord's body and blood, but also its inward power and effect.

All-gentle God, grant that my receiving of that body, taken from the Virgin Mary's womb by your Only-begotten Son, our Lord Jesus Christ, may fit me to become part of his mystical body and to be reckoned one of its members. Most loving Father, grant that your beloved Son whom I, an earthly wayfarer, am soon to receive in sacramental guise, may one day give me sight of his face and let me gaze on him for all eternity; who is God, living and reigning with you in the unity of the Holy Spirit for ever and ever. **Amen.** *Thomas Aquinas*

*The Lord's Prayer may be said.*

## The Conclusion

In peace we will lie down and sleep;
**for you alone, Lord, make us dwell in safety.**

Abide with us, Lord Jesus,
**for the night is at hand and the day is now past.**

As the night watch looks for the morning,
**so do we look for you, O Christ.**

Come with the dawning of the day
**and make yourself known in the breaking of the bread.**

The Lord bless us and watch over us;
the Lord make his face shine upon us and be gracious to
us;
the Lord look kindly on us and give us peace.
**Amen.**

# 11

# Form for the Admission of a Server

*(after a suitable period of training)*

*After the Greeting at the parish Eucharist those to be admitted are presented to the priest by the Head Server or another server.*

*Head Server*    Father, I present to you N.

*Priest*    Let us listen to the scriptures. Jesus said, 'whoever wants to become great among you must be your servant, and whoever wants to be first must be your slave – just as the Son of Man did not come to be served, but to serve, and to give his life as a ransom for many'. (Matthew 20.27–8 NIV)
What do you desire?

*Server*    I desire to be admitted to the work of a server in this church.

*Priest*    Are you prepared to commit yourself to this work on behalf of the Christian community; to give your time, your energy, and your concentration to it?

*Server*    I am, with the help of God.

*Priest*    I will go to the altar of God.

*Server*        To the God of my joy and gladness.

*Priest*        Let us pray. (*Silence*)

O God, our gracious Father, bless the servers of your church, that they may so serve before your earthly altar in reverence and holiness that they may attain, with all your saints and angels, the joy of serving you and worshipping you before your heavenly altar; through Jesus Christ our Lord. Amen.

N., I admit you as a server in this church. Perform your work with a cheerful heart, and may the Lord bless your going out and your coming in this day and for evermore.

*The server may receive his or her surplice or cotta and put it on. The newly admitted server should take a full part in the Eucharist which follows.*

# 12

# Prayers before Communion

I am the living bread which has come down from heaven. Anyone who eats this bread will live for ever; and the bread that I shall give is my flesh for the life of the world.                                   *John 6.51*

At this sacred banquet in which Christ is received, the memory of his passion is renewed, our minds are filled with grace and the promise of future glory is given to us.
*St Thomas Aquinas*

Lord Almighty, send down upon this Eucharist thy Holy Spirit. May he declare this bread that we shall eat to be the body of Christ, and this cup that we shall drink to be the blood of Christ. May he strengthen and sanctify us who eat this bread and drink this cup, grant forgiveness of our sins and deliver us from the wiles of the enemy. May he fill us with his presence and make us worthy of Christ, thy Son, and obtain for us eternal life. Amen.
*Adapted from the Apostolic Constitutions, fourth century*

We make Eucharist to you, Father, for the holy vine of David your servant, which you have revealed to us through your servant Jesus: glory to you for ever. We give thanks to you, Father, for the life and knowledge that you have given to us through your servant Jesus. May glory be yours for ever. As this bread was wheat scattered on the mountains, and was gathered to be one, so let your church be gathered from the ends of the Earth into your kingdom.               *From the Didache*

Come Lord, work on us, set us on fire and clasp us close, be fragrant to us, draw us to your love, let us run to you.                              *St Augustine*

# 13

# Priest's Prayers when Putting on the Vestments

*As he places the amice over his head, let him say:*

Lord, set the helmet of salvation on my head
to fend off all the assaults of the Evil One.

*As he puts on the alb:*

Purify me, Lord, and cleanse my heart,
so that, washed in the blood of the Lamb,
I may enjoy eternal bliss.

*As he ties the cincture:*

Lord, gird me about with the cincture of purity
and extinguish my fleshly desires,
that the virtue of continence and chastity may abide
within me.

*As he puts the stole around his neck:*

Lord, restore the stole of immortality
which I lost through the collusion of our first parents,

and, unworthy as I am to approach your sacred mysteries,
may I yet gain eternal joy.

*As he assumes the chasuble:*

Lord, you said, 'my yoke is easy and my burden is light';
Grant that I may be able to wear this vestment
so as to obtain your grace. Amen.

*The deacon says this prayer as he puts on the dalmatic:*

Lord, endow me with the garment of salvation
and the vestment of joy,
and with the dalmatic of justice
ever encompass me.

# 14

# Vestry Prayers before the Eucharist

| | |
|---|---|
| *President* | ✠ In the name of the Father, and of the Son, and of the Holy Spirit. |
| **All** | **Amen.** |

| | |
|---|---|
| *President* | My help comes from the Lord |
| *Servers* | **who has made heaven and earth.** |

| | |
|---|---|
| *President* | Teach me to do your will |
| *Servers* | **for you are my God.** |

| | |
|---|---|
| *President* | O send out your light and your truth |
| *Servers* | **and let them lead me.** |

| | |
|---|---|
| *President* | Father, your Son Jesus Christ gave his body to be broken on the cross; as in this Eucharist we share his broken body and become united with him, so may all your church be brought together into your kingdom; through the same Jesus Christ our Lord. |
| *All* | **Amen.** |

| | |
|---|---|
| *President* | I shall go to the altar of God, |
| *Servers* | **to God my joy and my delight.** |

*All bow to the crucifix and the Entrance Procession is formed.*

# Bibliography and Suggestions for Further Reading

## General Interest

P. F. Bradshaw (ed.), *The New SCM Dictionary of Liturgy and Worship*, SCM Press, 2002.

Cheslyn Jones, Geoffrey Wainwright and Edward Yarnold, SJ (eds), *The Study of Liturgy*, SPCK, 2nd edition, 1992.

J. C. J. Metford, *Dictionary of Christian Lore and Legend*, Thames and Hudson, 1983.

## On Liturgical Renewal

Edward Dowler and Brendan Clover, *An Everlasting Gift*, Canterbury Press, 2004.

Richard Giles, *Creating Uncommon Worship*, Canterbury Press, 2004.

Richard Giles, *Re-pitching the Tent*, Canterbury Press, 3rd edition, 2004.

## On Ceremonial

Peter Elliott, *Ceremonies of the Modern Roman Rite*, Ignatius Press, 1995.

*General Instruction on the Roman Missal*, Catholic Truth Society.

E. C. R. Lamburn, *Anglican Services*, W. Knott & Son, 2nd edition, 1963.

E. C. R. Lamburn, *Ritual Notes*, W. Knott & Son, 11th edition, 1964.

# Glossary

| | |
|---|---|
| **ambo** | A solid reading desk, usually made of stone. |
| **banners** | Many churches have banners of their patron saint, of the Blessed Virgin Mary, or of the Holy Eucharist. Some churches have banners of guilds and the Mothers' Union. |
| **canopy** | A rectangular fabric canopy with poles in each of its four corners is used in processions of the Sacrament. Some churches have an ombrellino, a liturgical umbrella, for this purpose. |
| **chancel, choir** | The eastern part of the church, originally separated from the nave by a screen. The choir seating was located in the chancel, and the high altar and sanctuary. |
| **chalice** | The silver or gold cup used for the communion of the priest and the laity. |
| **ciborium** | A covered bowl of gold or silver to contain the hosts (wafers of bread) for the communion of the people. |
| **Common Worship** | The new services of the Church of England. |
| **corporal** | A square white cloth folded in nine so as to contain any fragment of the body (*corpus*) of Christ. |
| **crib** | Most churches have a Christmas crib. St Francis of Assisi brought about the tradition, so that every church could have Bethlehem in its midst. |
| **crozier** | The crozier (or pastoral staff) is the symbol of the jurisdiction of the bishop. It can be made |

of wood or metal, can be highly decorated or simple. The diocesan bishop uses it in his diocese. Visiting bishops, other than a suffragan or assistant bishop, do not use it when not in their dioceses.

**day of obligation**  Days when the faithful are encouraged to make their communion. These include every Sunday and festivals.

**Eucharist**  Another name for the service of Holy Communion or the Mass. It comes from the Greek verb for 'give thanks'.

**humeral veil**  A large rectangle of cloth, often elaborately worked, with a clasp or morse. Used at Benediction, it is worn as a mark of respect to the Sacrament, the officiant covering his hands with the cloth before holding the monstrance or ciborium.

**lavabo**  The ceremonial washing of hands. The word comes from the latin verb for 'wash'.

**mitre**  The bishop's headgear. The two bands of cloth which hang down from its back are called fanons.

**morse**  A clasp that secures the two edges of the cape, often made of metal, and elaborately jewelled.

**nave**  A word which comes from the Latin *navis*, which means a ship. The nave is the central section of the church containing the congregational seating.

**officiant**  The priest who officiates at the service.

**oils**  Three holy oils are used in church services and pastorally: the oil of baptism, the oil of the sick, and the oil of chrism. Chrism takes its name from Christ, the Anointed One.

**Pall**  (1) A fabric-covered stiff card which is placed over the chalice to protect its contents from dust and insects. The pall is symbolic of the stone which was placed at the entrance to the tomb of Jesus.

(2) The large cloth which covers a coffin.

**palms**          Carried in procession on Palm Sunday. They are burnt to make the ashes for the following Ash Wednesday.

**Paschal**          The Easter candle blessed at the Easter Vigil.
**Candle**          It may be elaborately decorated and will have the year as part of the decoration. Five grains of incense may be inserted into it when it is blessed as a reminder of the five wounds of Jesus on the cross. Sometimes these grains of incense are put into a small metal (usually brass) container with a spike on it.

**paten**          A small dish or plate made of precious metal on which is placed the priest's host and small numbers of hosts for the people. The modern trend is for deeper and larger patens than before.

**pulpit**          The elevated structure which may be used for the delivery of sermons. Often the pulpit will have a soundboard or tester above it.

**purificator**          A rectangular cloth, folded in three lengthways, which is used to wipe, or purify, the chalice.

**quire**          See Choir.

**sacring bell**          The bell located close to the sacristy, used to notify the faithful that a service is about to begin.

**sanctuary**          Lamps which hang before an altar or a statue
**lamp**          or shrine. Red lamps are found at altars and statues other than statues of Our Lady, which have blue lamps. A white lamp burns before the Sacrament: this lamp is sometimes red, as in Roman Catholic churches.

**transept**          The areas at right angles to the nave in cruciform churches.

# Last Word

The Church exists first of all by and for the worship of Almighty God. Christian people are called to lose themselves in the mystery and wonder of the Creator, the Redeemer and the Sustainer in the liturgy of the Church. All else flows from this premise: community; social concern and pastoral care; concerns for peace and justice. Worship is fundamental.

Those who have a public part to play in the worship of the Church therefore need to keep this ever before them. Many have found their lives changed by their involvement in the liturgy, so the liturgy is part of the evangelistic outreach of the Church.

In the liturgy servers have a special part to play which we have tried to describe. Our words are certainly not the last word on the matter, but we hope they help. The last words must be that 'all should be done to the glory of God, Father, Son and Holy Spirit'.

# Index

Lightning Source UK Ltd.
Milton Keynes UK
UKHW021937170120
357166UK00012B/499

9 781853 116384